# THE MIGHTY VOLCANO

**by Cynthia Benjamin • illustrated by Berney Knox**

## Chapters

**Harcourt**

Orlando   Boston   Dallas   Chicago   San Diego

Visit *The Learning Site!*

**www.harcourtschool.com**

# The Making of a Volcano

Volcanoes are amazing forces of nature. A volcano is an opening in the earth through which hot gases, pieces of rock, and liquid rock burst into the air. Volcanoes were found all over the world millions of years ago. In fact, one theory blames volcanoes for the death of the dinosaurs. Some scientists think that after many volcanic eruptions, the earth was covered with volcanic gas and dust. Because of all that gas and dust, it became extremely cold. The extreme cold weather caused other environmental changes that made the dinosaurs die out.

## *Deep Inside the Earth*

A volcanic eruption begins deep inside the earth, where *magma*, or melted rock, is found. The rock melts because of the high temperatures in the earth's interior. Magma mixes with gas and slowly rises, forming a large pool, or chamber, called a *magma chamber*.

**Stromboli Volcano**

## When a Volcano Explodes

A volcanic eruption takes place when a volcano explodes. First, the magma, which is filled with gas, blasts a passageway through the weakened rock. This passageway is shaped like a cylinder. Then the magma moves through this passageway to the surface of the earth. At the surface, the gas and magma may shoot into the air through an opening at the top of the passageway. Sometimes the gas and magma escape through an opening in

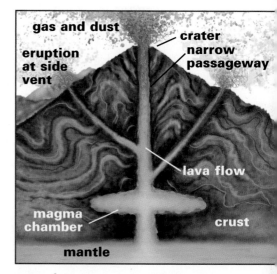

the side of the volcano. After the magma escapes to the surface, it's called *lava*.

When the magma and other materials pile up around the opening, a large volcano is created.

A volcanic eruption is an amazing sight. Red-hot lava flows quickly down the sides of the volcano like a river of fire. Volcanic gas, dust, and ash also explode into the air. Volcanic *dust* is made up of microscopic particles. Volcanic *ash* is made up of much larger particles.

## Where and Why Volcanoes Occur

### *The Ring of Fire*

The Ring of Fire is the name given to the belt of volcanic activity that circles the Pacific Ocean. Most volcanoes are found in the Ring of Fire. However, there are also volcanoes in other places in the world—including the bottom of the sea.

Some of the volcanoes in the Ring of Fire have been quiet, or *dormant,* for centuries. Others are *active* volcanoes. Active volcanoes erupt, sending giant fountains of burning rock into the air.

Earthquakes are also common along the Ring of Fire.

### Why Volcanoes Form in Certain Places

Think of the surface of the earth as a giant jigsaw puzzle. Instead of being made of cardboard, the earth's surface is made up of huge sections of rock, about 20 miles thick, called *plates*. These plates move because they rest on soft, hot rock deep inside the earth's interior. Sometimes the plates collide, or hit each other. Sometimes they spread apart, and sometimes

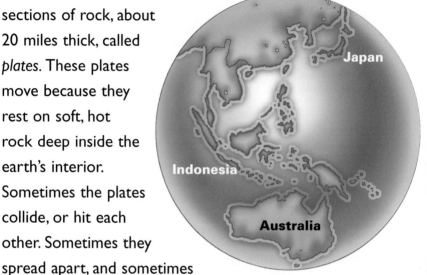

they slide past each other. When two plates collide, one plate is forced under the other. As a plate sinks, part of it melts and rises as magma, which eventually reaches the earth's surface and forms a volcano.

Most volcanoes are formed because two plates collide with each other. For example, Indonesia, which has about 125 active volcanoes, is at the edge of several plates. Japan is in the Ring of Fire, and it has 70 volcanoes. However, there are no volcanoes in Australia, which is in the middle of a plate.

### Indian Ocean

Today, if you sail through the Straits of Java (see map), you will see a strange sight. Small volcanoes light up the sky at night with a bright orange light.

In 1883 in the Indian Ocean, a volcanic island exploded, and the top of the volcano sank beneath the surface of the water. The volcanic island was Krakatoa, and its sinking caused huge waves that hit nearby islands and killed more than 36,000 people. All that was left of Krakatoa was a huge crater.

Then, in 1927, another volcanic island suddenly came to the surface in the Indian Ocean. It appeared in the same spot where Krakatoa had been. It was named Anak Krakatoa, which means "Child of Krakatoa."

## Atlantic Ocean

Iceland is a large island in the Atlantic Ocean where the winter snow rarely melts. Yet this cold land was actually formed by volcanic lava. This lava came from a crack in the ocean floor where two plates moved apart. As the lava cooled in layers, it formed an island of dark gray rock.

In 1963, fishers were actually able to watch the creation of a volcanic island near the coast of Iceland. First, the ocean began to boil. Then a black cone shape rose from the water. It had been formed by an underwater volcanic eruption. When the sea water rushed into the opening in the top of the volcano, a large cloud of steam rose from the island. The new island was named Surtsey, after a giant in Icelandic legends.

**A volcano erupting on the volcanic island of Surtsey, Iceland**

**Explosion of Mount Saint Helens in Washington State**

## *North America*

On May 18, 1980, Mount Saint Helens in Washington State exploded, blowing off the top of the mountain. People heard the noise 200 miles to the north in Vancouver, Canada. The volcano hadn't been active for almost 125 years.

Hot magma had risen under Mount Saint Helens and collected in an underground pool. Then it was carried to the surface through a long tube. The pressure continued to build until it was released by a huge explosion.

The avalanche of rocks was followed by a cloud of hot ash and gas that burnt everything in its path. This cloud was not transparent; it was greenish-brown, and survivors had to struggle to make their way through it. The volcanic explosion continued for nine hours.

## Pacific Ocean

The Hawai'ian Islands in the Pacific Ocean are volcanoes. However, they weren't formed when plates collided or separated. Instead, these volcanoes were formed above a *hot spot*.

When islands form in this way, melted rock pushes through the plate under the ocean floor and forms volcanoes. Then as the plate underneath the volcanoes slowly moves, they move away from the hot spot and stop erupting. Finally, new volcanoes form above the hot spot. As a result, a chain of islands, such as the Hawai'ian Islands, is created. These islands are really the tips of a large mountain range deep under the ocean. The Hawai'ian chain of volcanic islands stretches for 1,500 miles across the central Pacific Ocean.

**Mauna Kea, a Hawaiian volcano**

Volcanic eruption on Iceland in the Mid-Atlantic Ridge

## Underwater Volcanoes

### Mid-Ocean Ridges

Underwater volcanic mountain ranges that are formed on the ocean floor are called *mid-ocean ridges*. These underwater volcanoes are formed at the cracks on the ocean floor where two plates meet. When the plates move apart, red-hot magma moves up from deep within the earth.

New rock plugs up the space made when the plates pull apart and builds up the ocean floor. It forms ridges as it hardens. The melted rock also piles up in high cones and forms underwater volcanoes. Some of these volcanoes can become cone-shaped volcanic islands.

## Mid-Atlantic Ridge

One example of a mid-ocean ridge is the *Mid-Atlantic Ridge*. This is an underwater mountain range in the Atlantic Ocean. Iceland and the surrounding volcanic islands are part of this ridge.

## The Ocean Floor Widens

As plates pull apart and new rock fills the space between them, the sea floor spreads and some oceans grow each year. The mid-ocean ridge that runs through the Red Sea has created new ocean floor for about 20 million years. Because the ocean floor is spreading, Arabia is actually moving away from Africa.

However, while some oceans are becoming wider, the Pacific Ocean is getting smaller. In the same way, the Mediterranean was once an ocean and is now a sea. In the distant future, as the plates close up, the Mediterranean Sea will disappear completely and a mountain range will take its place.

## Famous Volcanoes of the Past

When nature runs wild, volcanoes are one result. Close your eyes and go back in time to August 24, A.D. 79. Imagine living in the wealthy Roman town of Pompeii, home to 200,000 people. You dimly remember the earthquake that destroyed parts of Pompeii and the nearby town of Herculaneum seventeen years ago. Suddenly you hear a loud, rumbling sound. You rush from your house into the street. Soon you are joined by hundreds of your neighbors. Mount Vesuvius, a volcano near Pompeii, has erupted. As you run, a storm of stones falls, and you struggle not to breathe in the deadly gas. If you thought you were safe from wild nature, you were wrong!

Herculaneum

▲Mt. Vesuvius

• •Pompeii

We now know a great deal about the eruption of Mount Vesuvius. A famous Roman writer who saw it described the explosion in a letter. Also, archaeologists have dug up the remains of both Pompeii and Herculaneum. They have even made plaster casts of the bodies of people and animals that were found there. Their hard work has given us valuable information about how the people in these towns lived and died.

Tourists visit the ruins of Pompeii.

In Pompeii many people were able to escape; however, more than 2,000 citizens died. They were killed by the deadly blast of gas and ash that flowed from the volcano. The huge ash cloud that covered Pompeii missed Herculaneum, which was west of the volcano. However, a flow of hot ash, rock, and volcanic material buried the town up to 65 feet deep in some places.

## Learning About Volcanoes

Volcanoes have terrified people for centuries. To explain them, cultures created traditional legends, myths, and folktales. Today, we have more scientific explanations for volcanoes.

A volcanologist

### Volcanologists

A scientist who watches, records, and interprets volcanoes is called a *volcanologist*. These scientists try to forecast when and how a volcano will erupt. They know that some volcanoes remain dormant with no volcanic activity for many years. However, a dormant volcano can still become active and erupt.

Volcanologists study information in their laboratories. They also collect lava and gas samples on the slopes of volcanoes. To protect themselves from the volcano's heat, they wear special clothing, including heavy gloves. Unfortunately, this suit makes the scientist unable to hear, see, or feel what is happening. Because the suit is so bulky, a volcanologist may not be able to run to safety in dangerous situations.

Volcanologists also use special equipment to do their job. A type of electric thermometer helps them take the

temperature of a lava flow. A tape measure is used to find out how much the cracks in the ground have widened. Another piece of equipment, called a level, can show small changes in the ground level.

**A volcanologist takes the temperature of a lava flow.**

# Volcanoes on Other Planets

Space missions have collected photographs and rock samples showing that volcanoes exist on other planets in the solar system. There are volcanoes on Mars and the moon that have been extinct, or inactive, for millions of years. The volcano Olympus Mons on Mars is 370 miles across at its base, and its crater is 40 miles wide. It is the largest volcano in the solar system.

There has also been volcanic activity on Venus. The volcanoes on Venus were created by hot spots, just as the Hawai'ian islands on Earth were. Some volcanoes on Venus are still active and send clouds of gas into the sky.

There is also evidence of volcanic eruptions on Io, one of Jupiter's sixteen moons. In 1979 the *Voyager* space probe flew past Jupiter. It sent back pictures of the volcano Prometheus as it blasted gases 100 miles above the surface of Io.

Io, the innermost satellite of Jupiter. The black spots are associated with craters of possible volcanic origin.